MONSTERS!

# THE LOCH NESS MONSTER

BY FRANCES NAGLE

HOT TOPICS

Gareth Stevens PUBLISHING

**Please visit our website, www.garethstevens.com. For a free color catalog of all our high-quality books, call toll free 1-800-542-2595 or fax 1-877-542-2596.**

**Cataloging-in-Publication Data**

Names: Nagle, Frances.
Title: The Loch Ness monster / Frances Nagle.
Description: New York : Gareth Stevens Publishing, 2016. | Series: Monsters! | Includes index.
Identifiers: ISBN 9781482448634 (pbk.) | ISBN 9781482448658 (library bound) | ISBN 9781482448641 (6 pack)
Subjects: LCSH: Loch Ness monster--Juvenile literature.
Classification: LCC QL89.2.L6 N335 2016 | DDC 001.944--dc23

First Edition

Published in 2017 by
**Gareth Stevens Publishing**
111 East 14th Street, Suite 349
New York, NY 10003



Designer: Samantha DeMartin
Editor: Kristen Nelson

Photo credits: Cover, p. 1 Victor Habbick/Visuals Unlimited/Getty Images; pp. 5 (map), 30 Serban Bogdan/Shutterstock.com; p. 5 (main) Markus Gann/Shutterstock.com; p. 7 Barashkova Natalia/Shutterstock.com; p. 9 General Photographic Agency/Hulton Archive/Getty Images; p. 11 Ian Tyas/Hulton Archive/Getty Images; p. 13 Keystone-France/Gamma-Keystone/Getty Images; pp. 15, 27 Victor Habbick/Shutterstock.com; p. 17 Richard du Toit/Gallo Images/Getty Images; p. 19 Keystone/Hulton Archive/Getty Images; p. 21 Fox Photos/Hulton Archive/Getty Images; p. 23 Mark A. Rice/Shutterstock.com; p. 25 MichaelTaylor3d/Shutterstock.com; p. 26 Rolls Press/Popperfoto/Getty Images; p. 29 Education Images/Universal Images Group/Getty Images.



Printed in the United States of America

CPSIA compliance information: Batch #CS16GS: For further information contact Gareth Stevens, New York, New York at 1-800-542-2595.

# CONTENTS

# DEEP UNDERWATER

Loch Ness is almost 800 feet (245 m) deep, and its waters are cloudy. From the shore, it's impossible to see if something swims deep below the **surface**. Many people believe they've spotted a monster in it! Are they telling the truth?

## BEYOND THE MYTH

Loch Ness is in Scotland. It's the lake with the largest **volume** of freshwater in Great Britain!

# BUILT ON MYTH

**Myths** of monsters in Scotland's waters are quite old. Water horses, or kelpies, are said to be magical but evil. One story tells of children trying to ride a water horse and being taken into the water to their death!

## BEYOND THE MYTH

A monster in Loch Ness is included in a book from the seventh century about the life of Saint Columba.

# 1933

Modern ideas of the Loch Ness monster date back to April 1933. A couple said they saw a huge animal swimming near the loch's surface. On May 2, a newspaper reported a story about what the couple saw.

## BEYOND THE MYTH

In 1933, a new road was built on the shore of Loch Ness. It was the first time people could get a clear view of the loch.

Soon after, another couple said they saw a strange **creature** crossing the road by Loch Ness. Other newspapers started writing stories about the sightings. People began sitting by the loch and trying to spot the monster themselves!

## BEYOND THE MYTH

"Nessie" is a common name used for the Loch Ness monster. However, it was called "Bobby" for a time after the first sightings!

# Hunting for Nessie

Radio shows and newspapers offered money to the person who could catch the Loch Ness monster! One London newspaper hired a hunter named Marmaduke Wetherell to **capture** it first. He had **experience** hunting other large animals.

## BEYOND THE MYTH

Sightings of the Loch Ness monster said the animal had a huge body with a very long neck.

MARMADUKE WETHERELL (LEFT)

After a few days, Wetherell reported finding the footprints of a very large animal. He said it was likely 20 feet (6 m) long! He made **casts** of the footprints and sent them to the Natural History Museum in London, England.

## BEYOND THE MYTH

It was the Inverness *Courier* newspaper that first called the creature in Loch Ness a "monster."

# FAKE FOOTPRINTS

The zoologists at the Natural History Museum had bad news for Wetherell. The footprints came from a hippopotamus! It was believed someone made the footprints using a dried hippo foot.

## BEYOND THE MYTH

Zoologists study the lives of animals. Cryptozoologists are people who study creatures that haven't been proven real, such as Nessie.

# CAUGHT ON CAMERA

In 1934, a doctor named R. Kenneth Wilson took a picture that seemed to prove that the Loch Ness monster was real. The picture seems to show an animal's long neck above the surface of Loch Ness.

## BEYOND THE MYTH

—Wilson's picture was published in *London Daily Mail*. It shaped what people around the world thought the Loch Ness monster looked like.

Sixty years later, Wilson's picture was found to be fake! Wetherell, angry about what happened with the hippo footprints, set up the picture. He had Wilson sell the photo to the *Daily Mail* so no one would know he took it.

## BEYOND THE MYTH

In 1975, Wetherell's son Ian wrote the truth about how his father faked the picture. No one paid attention to this fact until Ian's stepbrother said it years later.

LOCH NESS INVESTIGATION
NSD 651

# STUDYING THE LOCH

In 1957, a book collecting thousands of reports of the Loch Ness monster came out. The sightings were from fisherman, teachers, and even someone who won a Nobel Prize! The book renewed interest in looking for the creature.

## BEYOND THE MYTH

People who don't believe in the Loch Ness monster say sightings may be because of seiches (SAY-shuz). Seiches are movements of the water's surface that happen when colder water flows into the warmer loch water.

Between the late 1950s and the mid-1970s, studies were done looking in the loch for an unknown creature. Several of these used sonar, which uses sound waves to find things in a body of water.

## BEYOND THE MYTH

The long-necked creature reported in Loch Ness was said by some to be the last of the plesiosaurs, a huge creature that died out 65 million years ago! No studies have supported this idea.

In 1975, a group used sonar and underwater photography in Loch Ness. They took a picture that seemed to have fins in it! Later, it was shown that the picture had been changed to look like that.

1975 PHOTO

## BEYOND THE MYTH

The bottom of Loch Ness is muddy, which helps make the water cloudy. It's hard to take a clear picture of anything.

# STILL ON THE LOOKOUT!

People still report seeing a strange animal in Loch Ness. Nothing has ever proven that the Loch Ness monster is swimming in the loch—but nothing has proven it isn't, either! Do you believe?

## BEYOND THE MYTH

Google set up a camera on the loch and underwater to try to find Nessie. They haven't found anything—yet.

# Loch Monsters!

Many other lochs in Scotland are said to be home to monsters. Loch Ness is just the most famous!

# FOR MORE INFORMATION

## BOOKS

Lassieur, Allison. *Is the Loch Ness Monster Real?* Mankato, MN: Amicus High Interest, 2016.

Rivkin, Jennifer. *Searching for the Loch Ness Monster.* New York, NY: PowerKids Press, 2015.

Turner, Tracy. *20 Beasts and Monsters.* Mankato, MN: Smart Apple Media, 2016.

## WEBSITES

**Legend of the Loch Ness Monster**

*animalplanet.com/tv-shows/weird-true-and-freaky/videos/legend-of-the-loch-ness/*

Watch a short video about a Loch Ness monster sighting.

**Nessie**

*learnenglishkids.britishcouncil.org/en/word-games/fill-the-gap/nessie*

How much do you know about the Loch Ness monster? Test it here!

**Publisher's note to educators and parents:** Our editors have carefully reviewed these websites to ensure that they are suitable for students. Many websites change frequently, however, and we cannot guarantee that a site's future contents will continue to meet our high standards of quality and educational value. Be advised that students should be closely supervised whenever they access the Internet.

# GLOSSARY

**capture:** to trap

**cast:** to make an object by pouring melted material into a mold and letting it harden

**creature:** an animallike being

**experience:** practice

**myth:** a story

**surface:** the top of a liquid

**volume:** a measurement of liquid that shows the amount of space it takes up

# INDEX

